MW00465656

SHORT ROMANTIC PIECES FO[

Edited by LIONEL SALTER

BOOK I

The pieces in this book are about Grades 1 and 2 in standard (Associated Board)
Metronome marks within square brackets are editorial

THE ASSOCIATED BOARD OF THE ROYAL SCHOOLS OF MUSIC

LESSON in C

DIABELLI, Op.125 No.6

A friend of Haydn's (and a pupil of his younger brother Michael), Anton Diabelli was a popular teacher and composer for the piano in Vienna, where he subsequently became a successful music publisher. Among the chief composers in his catalogue were Czerny and Schubert.

© 1986 by The Associated Board of the Royal Schools of Music.

AB 1898

STUDY in D

CZERNY, Op.777 No.15

Karl Czerny was a favourite pupil of Beethoven (who at one time contemplated living in his house) and the teacher of Liszt. Enormously prolific in almost every sphere of music, he is remembered today almost solely for his numerous educational works for piano.

AB 1898

4

COUNTRY DANCE

Although born in Coblenz, Franz Hünten studied in Paris (where he was a pupil of Cherubini) and became a fashionable piano teacher there. In his mid-forties he returned to his home town, where his two brothers also were successful piano teachers.

GERMAN DANCE

SCHUBERT, D.972 No.3

Schubert wrote over 400 dance pieces, many actually intended for his friends to dance to. This one is unusual in that it also constitutes the piano part of his song *Hänflings Liebeswerbung* ('The linnet's wooing').

ALLEGRO

H. WOHLFAHRT

The Leipzig teacher Heinrich Wohlfahrt wrote a number of educational treatises as well as a *Piano method for children* (1862), from which both these pieces are taken.

WALTZ in C

H. WOHLFAHRT

STUDY in A minor

F. BEYER, Op.101 No.93

A native of Mainz, Ferdinand Beyer was an employee of the publishing house of Schott in that town, for which he wrote large quantities of transcriptions, fantasias, potpourris, etc.

POLKA

GLINKA

In his youth Glinka took piano lessons from John Field in St Petersburg. Possessed of private means, he travelled extensively in Europe, but largely as a result of his operas *A Life for the Tsar* and *Ruslan and Lyudmila* he is regarded as the founder of the Russian nationalist school of composers. This *Polka* is precisely dated '12 April 1849'.

AB 1898

CATCH-ME-IF-YOU-CAN

SCHUMANN

Schumann wrote the *Album for the Young* primarily for his eldest child's seventh birthday: he enjoyed the task so much that he composed all the pieces in just over a fortnight. There were several more besides the 43 that were eventually published: here are two of them, which have been taken from the composer's sketches.

HIDE-AND-SEEK

SCHUMANN

Immer sehr leise [Sempre molto piano]

STUDY in A

LE COUPPEY, Op.17 No.7

This comes from *L'Alphabet*, one of a large number of educational albums by Félix le Couppey, who was a professor at the Paris Conservatoire (where he himself had been a pupil).

THE SCABIOUS FLOWER

HELLER, Op.138 No.14

Born in Pest, the Hungarian capital, Stephen Heller studied in Vienna and Augsburg but settled in Paris, where some critics considered him an even more poetic pianist than Chopin. He also had a large following in England.

THE BELLS

ALKAN, Op.63 No.4

On account of his many large-scale virtuoso keyboard works, Alkan (real name Morhange) has been called 'the Berlioz of the piano'. He was so precocious that he was admitted to the Paris Conservatoire at the age of six: he became very friendly with Chopin but spent much of his life in seclusion.

GRANDMOTHER'S SONG

VOLKMANN, Op.27 No.4

Greatly influenced by Schumann, Robert Volkmann composed much orchestral and chamber music, and taught in Prague, Vienna and Budapest. The collection of *Grandmother's songs* from which this piece comes was published in 1880.

STUDY in D

C. GURLITT, Op.187 No.51

A main influence on Cornelius Gurlitt was Schumann, whom he visited with his friend Carl Reinecke (the son of his teacher). Altona, where Gurlitt was born, was then Danish: after teaching in Copenhagen he became a professor at the Hamburg Conservatory. The *Study* comes from a collection of *Melodious Little Studies*: *Undismayed* from a volume of 12 pieces entitled *The Friend of the Family*.

AB 1898

UNDISMAYED

Allegretto [♩ = 116]

C. GURLITT, Op.197 No.7

A FAIRY STORY

("There was once a princess . . .")

Allegretto [♩. = 76]   KULLAK, Op.62 No.1

Theodor Kullak, one of a family of musicians, was a pupil of Czerny and became court pianist to the King of Prussia. He was a co-founder of a conservatory in Berlin in 1850, but, falling out with his partner, he set up a school of his own (also in Berlin) five years later.

AB 1898

GOING TO SLEEP

K. J. BISCHOFF, Op.31 No.2

In 1850 Kaspar Bischoff founded a choral society in Frankfurt, where he also won a prize for a string trio which included a movement in quintuple time (then still unusual). The album from which this piece is taken was written for his little daughter Mary.

AB 1898

PRELUDE

Andante [♩ = 120]

KIRCHNER, Op.65 No.2

One of Schumann's most gifted followers, Theodor Kirchner was successively an organist and conductor in Switzerland for 30 years, director of a music school in Würzburg, a teacher in Leipzig and a professor of chamber music in Dresden. Nearly all his compositions are for piano solo or duet: the album from which the *Vivace* is taken has the Schumannesque title *New Scenes of Childhood*.

AB 1898

VIVACE

KIRCHNER, Op.55 No.23

PRELUDE

REINECKE, from Op.183 No.1

After initial successes as a violinist, Carl Reinecke had a distinguished career as a pianist, conductor and composer. He was in turn court pianist in Copenhagen, a professor in Cologne, director of music in Breslau, for 35 years conductor of the Leipzig Gewandhaus and simultaneously, for even longer, taught at the Leipzig Conservatory.

AB 1898

A FAIRY TALE

REINECKE, from Op.127a No.6

CHILDREN'S MARCH

MERKEL, Op.31 No.1

For a time Gustav Merkel was a pupil of Schumann. He spent most of his life in Dresden, holding appointments as organist in various churches there and becoming court organist, a professor at the Conservatory and director of the Singakademie.

A ROMP

BRESLAUR, Op.46 No.32

Emil Breslaur's life was a busy one. Besides teaching in Berlin (where he founded a Teachers' Association) and editing a magazine on music education, he was also a synagogue cantor.

DANCE OF THE DRAGONFLIES

ROHDE, Op.76 No.7

Eduard Rohde was born in Halle and became a teacher in Berlin. His voluminous output consisted largely – apart from his piano music – of songs, folksong arrangements and motets.

AB 1898

MELODY

G. HASSE, Op.44 No.1

Little is known of Gustav Hasse; but besides his piano pieces he composed 175 songs.

OLD FRENCH SONG

TCHAIKOVSKY, Op.39 No.16

Molto moderato [♩ = c.84]

Tchaikovsky's Op.39 *Children's Album* was written in the country near Kiev 'as a relaxation', according to the composer, after completing his Fourth Symphony and the opera *Evgeny Onyegin*.

MELODY

Allegretto moderato [♩ = 116]

H. HOFMANN, Op.77 No.5

Heinrich Hofmann was a Berlin pianist and teacher who had considerable success in Germany with his orchestral works and operas. This piece comes from a volume of *Skizzen* ('Sketches').

TO MY LITTLE FRIENDS

SANDRÉ

Gustave Sandré was a French composer of songs, piano pieces and chamber works. These pieces are the 'dedication' and No.5 in the album *For the little ones*, which appeared as a supplement to the magazine *L'Illustration* at Christmas 1896.

AB 1898

DOWN IN THE DUMPS

SANDRÉ

Un peu lent, plaintif [♩ = 96]

HEARTACHE

R. FUCHS, Op.32 No.2

Calmly and expressively [♩ = 100]

Robert Fuchs, best known for his clarinet quintet and his fine Serenades for string orchestra, was an influential professor at the Vienna Conservatory, of which his elder brother later became director. Among his pupils were Mahler and Hugo Wolf.

AB 1898

THE LITTLE TRUMPETER

R. FUCHS, Op.32 No.4

GAVOTTE

STANFORD

Stanford, the most distinguished of Irish composers, studied for a time under Reinecke. He occupied a leading position in British musical life: he was conductor of the London Bach Choir and director of the Leeds Triennial Festival, but his greatest influence was as the professor of music at Cambridge and a teacher of composition at the Royal College of Music, both of which appointments he held for more than 30 years.

AB 1898

SCHERZO

STANFORD

INVENTION

LYAPUNOV

As a member of the Imperial Geographic Society, Lyapunov (who had studied with Tchaikovsky) collected and published nearly 300 folksongs from Russian provinces. After being assistant director of the Imperial Choir in St Petersburg and an inspector of music, he became a colleague of Maikapar on the staff of the Conservatory there; but after the Revolution he settled in Paris.

AB 1898

A SLIGHT MISUNDERSTANDING

LADUKHIN

Nikolai Ladukhin studied at the St Petersburg Conservatory and later became a professor there (when it then was renamed Leningrad).

AB 1898

MAZURKA

GRECHANINOV, Op.98 No.13

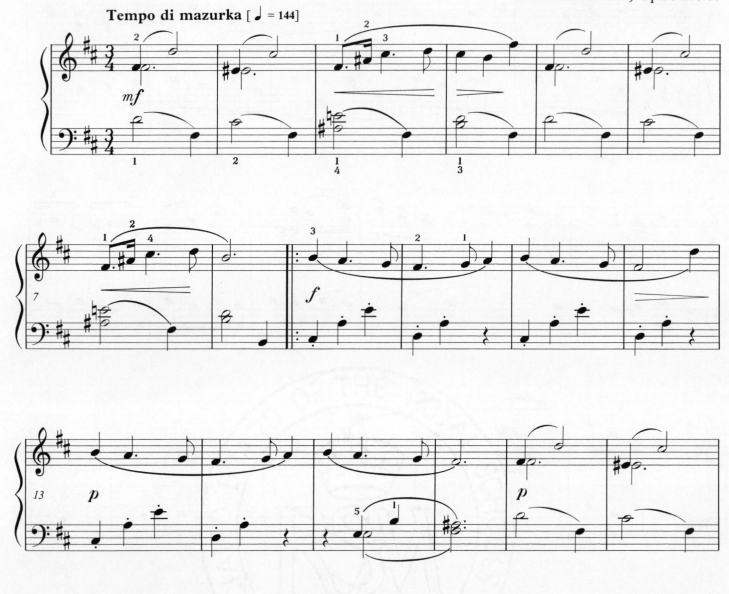

An extremely prolific composer in many fields of music (especially vocal and choral), Grechaninov had been a pupil of Arensky in Moscow and of Rimsky-Korsakov in St Petersburg. He earned a reputation as a conductor of his own works in Paris, where he lived for a time; but in 1939 he settled in New York and later became an American citizen.

AB 1898

A MINIATURE

MAIKAPAR, Op.4 No.3

Allegretto giocoso [♩ = 132]

For 20 years a professor at the St Petersburg Conservatory, where he himself had been a student, Samuil Maikapar had also been a pupil of the great piano teacher Leschetizky in Vienna. He wrote a large number of small pieces for the piano as well as studies for special aspects of piano technique. The original version of this piece is a semitone higher.

ALLEGRETTO

NIELSEN, Op.53 No.2

Carl Nielsen, the most significant composer Denmark has produced, was for some years conductor of the Royal Opera and of the Copenhagen Musical Society, and for a time director of the Conservatory there. His *Piano music for big and small* from which these two pieces are taken was written in the year before his death.

AB 1898

MARZIALE

NIELSEN, Op.53 No.7

SAD SONG

GEDIKE, Op.36 No.39

A fourth-generation member of a family of composers of German extraction, Alexander Gedike studied under Arensky in Moscow. He won the Rubinstein Prize in an international competition for composers in Vienna; wrote four operas to his own libretti, four concertos and three symphonies, as well as much piano music; and was also a professor of the piano and organ at the Moscow Conservatory.

AB 1898

NIGHT IN THE WOODS

GEDIKE, Op.36 No.32

SWAYING BRANCHES

DUNHILL

After studying with Stanford, Thomas Dunhill was, for ten years, a music master at Eton and, for much longer, a professor at the Royal College of Music. His breadth of taste enabled him to write distinguished chamber works and, at the other end of the musical spectrum, the very successful light opera *Tantivy Towers*.

Copyright 1935 by The Associated Board of the Royal Schools of Music

WALTZ

DYSON

George Dyson taught at a number of leading public schools, including Marlborough, Rugby, Wellington and Winchester, and then for fifteen years was director of the Royal College of Music (where he himself had been a student and had won the Mendelssohn Scholarship).

Copyright 1952 by The Associated Board of the Royal Schools of Music

LITTLE SONG

KABALEVSKY, Op.27 No.1

Though he has to his credit five operas, four symphonies and six concertos (three of them for young players), Kabalevsky is best known for his work in the educational field. After being appointed a professor at the Moscow Conservatory, he became head of a commission on the musical education of children and, later, president of the International Society for Musical Education.

AB 1898

WALTZ

Non troppo allegro [♩. = 60]

KABALEVSKY, Op. 39 No. 13

ALL FORLORN

ALWYN

For 30 years a professor of composition at the Royal Academy of Music, where he himself had studied, William Alwyn was a founder-member of the Composers' Guild of Great Britain. Besides five symphonies, two operas and three string quartets, he wrote a large number of distinguished film scores.

Copyright 1932 by The Associated Board of the Royal Schools of Music

AB 1898